EFFORTLESS READING

THE SIMPLE WAY TO READ AND GUARANTEE REMARKALBE RESULTS

VU TRAN

TABLE OF CONTENTS

A NOTE TO YOU, THE READER

In our overloaded lives, finding time to read is a true challenge. Yet, we occasionally hear great people, like Bill Gates, Warren Buffet, or Elon Musk, talk about how they maintain their reading routines or how their dedication to reading helps differentiate them from the crowd.

Perhaps, at a conference, you've heard someone intelligently quote a book, impressing the audience with their knowledge, and you would like to do the same.

You might have already read other self-development books on how to increase your reading speed. The problem, though, is that they all tend to offer pretty much the same advice: Expand your vision, stop your vocals, scan, skim, and so on. It's all good advice, but not especially new, and fails to address a fundamental dilemma of reading.

People still use the linear reading technique taught in elementary school to ingest global knowledge. And as this body of global knowledge exponentially increases, our typical manner of reading, the linear technique, won't help us keep pace.

This book is aimed at nonfiction readers who read under 50 books every year and want to up their game. Avid readers will also enjoy the book, as it provides a new perspective about reading habits. For entrepreneurs who are very tight on learning time, this book could be the remedy for your thirst for knowledge, helping you to keep your innovation-ball rolling on the industry's edge.

No matter where you are in your life right now, whether you are on top of your game or in the midst of adversity, struggling to find your way—I know there is at least one common thing we share: humility in seeking true self-improvement, not just entertainment, from reading.

Effortless Reading provides a new approach to reading that once again puts you in control of the exponentially growing knowledge stream, supporting you in achieving the level of success that you desire. Even if you are a slow reader, you can still apply the technique proposed in *Effortless Reading*. If you have never read any book before, following the formula in *Effortless Reading* will save you months of wasteful reading effort.

The best part—you can spend as few as 15 minutes a day and still be able to build a sustainable and beneficial reading practice.

As a dedicated student of human potentials with a particular focus on reading, I've learned and tested many reading techniques from Tony Buzan's classic speed-reading to the ultimate page-flipping hustle of PhotoReading. I can say with absolute certainty that *Effortless Reading* is the most practical, results-oriented reading method that I have ever encountered. It will improve any—and every—aspect of your reading, and you will learn faster than you believed possible.

In this book, you'll come across the following:

- Fundamentals of the reading mindset that distinguish a smart reader from a regular one.
- Pitfalls that stop people from building healthy reading habits.
- The recommended reading approach and the four elements those make it efficient and effortless.

You might have realized that with today's deluge of information, you have to do something different to keep up. Otherwise, you may be passed by others who are more informed. Mastering the deluge is exactly what we will be doing here.

My approach, called "deliberated reading," may sound counterintuitive at first, but it works. And it works because the new age of rich media and information forces us to reevaluate and change our traditional reading method.

I promise that if you follow the reading approach offered in this book, you will read three times as much as you currently do without any decrease in the quality of your comprehension. For the same book, it will cut your reading time in half, so you can spend that additional time with your friends and family, or invest it in yourself.

Effortless Reading is intended to be concise, addressing only the essential elements needed for your reading journey. My goal is for you to finish this book in one 30-minute session and revisit sections later to dive more deeply into particular aspects.

To ensure you find the most value out of this book, I avoid discussing the traditional techniques associated with speed-reading. However, I include a review of those techniques in the review section that you can download and review at http://effortless-reading.com/resources.

Before you jump in, I'd like to share with you something to keep in mind while reading the book. It is the one thing that differentiates the elite from the rest.

As my mentor, Jim Rohn, stated, "What is easy to do, is easy not to do." Although the principles mentioned in this book are simple, only your TAKING ACTION can put them into use.

Only people who invest resources in building up their knowledge, one step at a time, can achieve extraordinary results.

So stop putting this off, learn the technique, and take control of your knowledge—now.

INTRODUCTION

HOW IT ALL BEGAN

I grew up in Vietnam, a developing country, in which a young person's educational record at school impacts his or her whole life, including social status and career path. A favorite subject of Vietnamese parents is discussing how well their children are doing at school, if they are studying extra hours, going to after-school tutorials, and so on.

In my country, until you're eighteen, your one and only goal is to get your foot into the door of a good college. Young people do it by studying 60+ hours every week. They need to train hard to compete with the 300,000 other candidates every year in the grand college entrance exam. A single student's chance of winning is 1:5 for a midrange college and 1:10, or sometimes even 1:20, for the top colleges.

In Vietnam, education greatly determines social status. No matter if the students are rich or poor, if they can't get into college by age 18, they are doomed. The society classifies those unlucky people as members of the lowest class called— the uneducated or the failures. Even worse, it's not just them, but their families too that bear that label.

Like most children raised in such an environment, I was competitive. My parents trained me to be so. Reading was one of the activities they emphasized.

At that time, reading was very underrated. Teenagers spent 80% of their time going to school and studying extra hours until late at night. They barely had time for any hobbies, so reading was rarely on the calendar.

I was lucky to get exposed to reading early on. My parents were the first to introduce me to personal development genre, with *Study Smarter, Not Harder* book. I doubt my parents understand how impactful that act was, but I'm grateful they set me on the path to success.

Once in high school, I became addicted to life hacking. I would go as far as possible to learn how to read faster and memorize better. My favorite books, written by Tony Buzan, addressed speed-reading, mastering memory, mind mapping, and much more.

I mastered many (traditional) speed-reading techniques, including enlarging my eye vision, stopping vocalizing, scanning, and skimming. Speed-reading was my favorite. At a young age, my reading speed was about 30 pages per hour (around 300 words per minute), and I normally read 30 books in a year.

THE DIP

Around September 2012, my reading hit its plateau point. No matter how many books I read, I couldn't seem to move an inch. I got hit by a mystery force; I just couldn't get better. Later on, I figured out I was hit by "the dip."

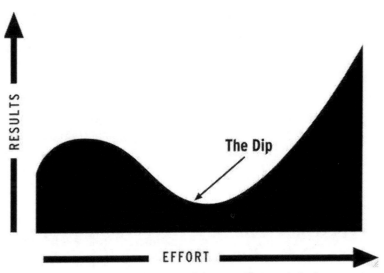

The Dip: The long stretch between beginner's luck and real accomplishment

Seth Godin describes "the dip" in his book with the same title as "the long slog between starting and mastery," "the difference between the easy beginner's technique and the more useful expert approach in skiing or fashion design," and "the long stretch between beginner's luck and real accomplishment."

Essentially "the dip" is when things get harder and less fun. When you hit the bottom of "the dip," things get really hard, and it's not much fun at all.

In an attempt to crawl out of the dip, I made an investment in a three-day reading course. The class was called "PhotoReading." Ironically, I was suspicious of the strange reading method offered in this course. It was not a normal speed-reading class. It was not easy to execute either. At some level, it was like a religion in that you had to believe in its practices, and it was hard to measure.

PhotoReading is a technique that relies on the unconscious mind to read through a book. When you see someone rapidly flipping through pages of a book and they are able to recall facts or even paragraphs from the book, you are observing PhotoReading. A 300-page book can be read in five minutes using this technique.

The challenge about PhotoReading is you have to train your conscious mind to relax and leave the rest to your unconscious, trusting it will do the job to read all the "photos" captured. The hard part is that the you have to believe that the conscious mind will, somehow, "incubate" the picture (of the page) over a period of time. Then, you can recall or invoke the information using some trigger keywords.

This technique requires a considerable amount of practice before seeing any effect, similar to someone first practicing yoga or mediation.

While I was not able to master PhotoReading, I learned two concepts that later became the foundation of "deliberated reading," the method I developed and present in this book:
1. Get through the book in multiple passes—each with a different purpose, speed, and comprehensive level.
2. Learn to let go and feel comfortable with missing (not reading) some pages of the book.

In that year, I increased my speed to 50 pages per hour. As I finished the eightieth book (for that year), I landed myself a six-figure salary job at Amazon.

THE BOOK—*NOT* READ—WON'T HELP

I learned the true value of book knowledge only after I failed in my first startup, burning $20,000 along the way. One evening in late December 2013, I was desperate, with my business in free fall. Surfing the web for advice led me to *Nail It Then Scale It* by Nathan Furr and Paul Ahlstrom. The cover of the book said it all—"Most entrepreneurs fail because they do the right thing, but in the wrong ORDER." In my case, I did not "nail" the market fit and prematurely "scaled" my startup by spending countless efforts and resources in marketing.

I spent the rest of the night finishing the book. As I made it through half of it, I started crying—had I read this book nine months previously, I probably would have been in much better shape with my startup . . .

This taught me that reading one idea, in one book, at the right time, in the proper context, has a much greater impact than reading ten books at an unrelated time. I will dive into more details on this at a later stage in the book.

THE MAN WHO READ 5,000 BOOKS

Moving on from the failed startup, I started doing extensive training and reading again. My goal was to finish 52 books in the next year, boosting my knowledge and readying me for the next venture. Fifty-two would have been the number, if only I had not bumped into Tai Lopez, a multi-millionaire and motivational speaker, who later on became my mentor and taught me to read a book a day.

The fact that he read over 5,000 books in a few years' time

completely broke my limited belief in the number of books a human being can read. In my record of people who read, this guy is off the chart.

After learning his reading approach, called "smart reading," I was able to connect various techniques I had learned in the last five years and develop them into my own approach, called "deliberated reading." And it is this approach which I present to you over the course of this book.

In the next chapter, I present misconceptions and pitfalls about reading to make sure you best use your time while reading. Then, I will walk you through "deliberated reading," what it is and how to put it into practice to learn to read three times as fast as you do now.

CHAPTER 1
WHAT IS YOUR WHY?

Survival machines that can simulate the future are one jump ahead of survival machines who can only learn on the basis of overt trial and error.

The trouble with overt trial is that it takes time and energy.

The trouble with overt error is that it is often fatal.

Simulation is both safer and faster.
> — **Richard Dawkins** in *The Selfish Gene*

* * *

IF YOU COULD RECALL...

Choose any book you've purchased—can you recall why you started reading the book? When you bought the book, was there a compelling question that you wanted answered? Was it a burning question that your mind was curious about, so you were willing to trade money for that piece of knowledge, believing it would give a positive return on investment by your owning and reading the book? Your motivation to read it could have been that you were interested in the subject. Or maybe many people, whom you're following, kept mentioning the book, so you just had to get it.

Over the past year, I learned to ask myself better questions,

14

and one of the best questions is: *Do I stop reading a book once it has fulfilled my curiosity? Do I stop once the book has answered my question? If not, why?*

Most people don't simply stop reading a book once it has answered their questions. They get addicted to the idea of finishing the book.

As they read, their minds turn to the default mode, one in which the mind is constantly seeking new, fresh knowledge, regardless whether or not that knowledge is aligned with the person's original purpose for reading. The dopamine generated in reading creates an addiction that keeps them going. The result is that after a few hours spent on a book, they don't feel they have learned enough from the book as they had hoped.

The ability to control this default mode is what differentiates competent readers from the rest. Competent readers never let their minds fall into the default mode. They read with purpose and intention. They follow the "deliberate reading" approach presented in this book.

So keep in mind your why while going through the book.

Before we jump in the main content, I want to warn you: Don't be black and white about what to read or not read, meaning don't either read something to the end or not read it at all. Know that there's a gray area, an in-between place too.

If you look around, there are tons of people who haven't read a single book in years. And there are people who read, but are not successful in their lives. I am sure there's even examples of successful people who don't read. However, I can also show you even more examples of extraordinary people who read lots and use what they learn from reading to make their way to the top.

Without going further to convince you why you should read or should read even more, I want to share with you my mentor's teaching on the same topic. He has done such a good job explaining, that I want to give it directly to you without my words weighing in.

TAI LOPEZ ON WHY PEOPLE SHOULD READ

"We both understand the intrinsic value of being able to take in the wisdom, knowledge, and experience of the world's smartest people, whether they are alive (and too busy to meet with us in person) or whether they are dead. We want to know what they know.

"And you will run into the people that say books are not important. I suggest you ignore those people because there's no evidence that it is true. There's little evidence, and there is much evidence that almost every person who has the impact, who rises above the ground—which I'm sure you're inspired to do—whether it's Einstein, Tesla, or Bill Gates, they all say books have played an important role.

"Taking in the knowledge of other people is what Dr. Richard Dawkins in the book *Selfish Gene* called simulation. Simulation is the most powerful tool. We have the ability to watch somebody else put his or her hand in the fire and get burned. And go, 'I don't have to put my hand in the fire because I have the brain that tells me, if I do the same thing that person does, I will get the same (unwanted) result.'

"And we learn faster. You want to shave decades off the learning curve. Don't be mistaken. The smartest people spend 20–30 years learning, and the average people might take a lifetime. But if you ask them, they would say half of that time was wasted, doing the thing that they could have learned from other people.

"You should stand on the shoulder of the giant, and not waste your life figuring out things that have already been figured out.

"Unfortunately, the reason most people don't get what they want out of life is because they spend the majority of their life not simulating through the experience of people, but try to do it themselves, making mistakes themselves.

"What Dr. Richard Dawkins says in the book, is that trials can be costly in terms of time, and too much error is deadly. Whether it's your hope and dream, you can physically die or mentally die. If you don't know stuff, there's tremendous pain associated with that ignorance.

"In the world of 7-billion people combined with increasing complexity, the pace of the learning is growing so rapidly that the greatest skill you can have is the ability to get through the materials quickly."

Tai Lopez is right. In this increasingly complicated world, the greatest skill is to absorb knowledge as quickly as possible.

In order to accomplish that, we need both the right skills and philosophy. In the next chapter, we will go over the "skill" part once, from end to end. Then we'll dive deeply into the reasoning behind each element of the technique.

CHAPTER 2
YOUR READING CHEAT SHEET

This chapter lays out the details, the when, where, and how, on the deliberated reading approach and can be used as a "cheat sheet" in your second pass through this book.

There are three important aspects in regard to reading:
- Understanding your strength and your situation
- Activating the "gold miner mindset," reading with the "one thing" principle.
- Building your reading habit around your situation, goal, and available cognition.

WHEN TO READ?
You should read every day. The best time is in the morning before breakfast and in the evening, after dinner. Before breakfast, you are less likely to be interrupted than later in the day. Your supply of willpower is fresh after a good night's sleep, so you are naturally in an openness stage, ready to obtain new knowledge.

After dinner is a great time for stories with family and friends. It's a time that feels slow and best for easy-to-digest types of book, such as biographies or some quick how-to books. Reading after dinner plants a creative seed for the next day. It defuses your mind from being pragmatic while preparing you for a good night's sleep.

In *The Miracle Morning*, Hal Elrod identifies reading as one of the six things that successful people do in their morning ritual. Elrod explains that reading is an investment in your brain for your future.

WHAT DO YOU NEED?

Have a bookmark, a pen to mark or circle, a physical book, and a timer.

A physical book is preferable to an e-book. However, if you are reading an e-book, ensure your reading device allows the capturing of notes and bookmarking.

HOW MUCH TIME DO YOU NEED?

You will need 10 to 15 minutes for a single pass.

HOW SHOULD YOU POSITION YOURSELF?

Dr. Daniel Lieberman, a Harvard Professor, said sitting is not part of the natural physiology of the human body. A better position is to lie down and put your feet up on a chair, so that your legs are parallel to the ground. You might not be able to do this all the time, but try to be in that posture whenever you can.

In the following description of deliberated reading, I will use an example of reading the book, *The One Thing*, by Gary Keller.

The first step is to ask: *What is my end goal in reading this book?* The answer to this question corresponds with the first of the three aspects in reading: *Reading needs to start with an intention.* If you meet the author, what is the one question that you want to ask him or her?

Gary Keller spent more than 10 years building his top-rated US real estate company. In The One Thing, Keller gives key information to help the reader build a successful real estate business. I am aware that it is impossible to learn everything from him in 15 minutes of reading. More importantly though, if I try to capture everything from his whole book and put it all into practice, I would end up applying nothing after a few days.

So I will aim to gather only one golden nugget from his book, which corresponds with the second aspect of reading, i.e., activating the "gold miner mindset" and reading with the "one thing" principle.

Start by reading the book jacket. Learn more about the author and unblock your authority bias.

Our brain has developed strong filter layers for insignificant matters, and authority bias is one of them. How the authority bias works is that your brain quietly tells you, "I will not trust the information in the book unless the author is seen as expert in this subject." Learning about the author from the book jacket breaks down that bias.

Also note the year the book was published. The primary stream of thought of particular time periods can be significantly different and might impact the book. A finance book written in a time of recession might not be applicable during a time of expansion and vice versa.

Next, read the table of contents. Read the introduction and skim through the first chapter. Then figure out

which chapter will most likely fulfill what you are trying to acquire.

Check your time. You have probably spent about 5–7 minutes going through those initial steps. **Estimate how much time you can continue and how many pages you can go through.** Then start reading the chapter you have chosen. Use your natural speed, and bump it up a little bit if you find the content is not too dense.

The goal here is neither to speed-read nor to "read everything" in a short period of time. But rather, to pick one chapter and dive deeply into it at your own comfortable pace.

As you read, circle and underline the relevant ideas. Mark significant paragraphs with a star or any symbol that you like. You can write the significant idea on the back or the front of the book, where typically there are blank pages. Eventually, you should be able to develop your own annotation code system to support your reading.

Here is the most challenging part. After the time is up and you've finished the chapter you wanted to read—**let the book go.**

Say to yourself, "You know what, it's okay. I got enough from this book. I'm walking away from it, and I'm not afraid of missing anything. I will put the book in the back of my mind, knowing that it will always be there when I need it. I will remember if there's time, I can revisit the book."

In the table of contents, check off the chapter you read. If you haven't already, start a book list, recording all the titles you've read/passed through. Remember—maintaining a list of books is critical to track and form your reading habits.

In describing the overall approach to deliberated reading, you should notice that the three aspects, given in the opening of this chapter, all come into play. The first aspect, "understanding your strength and your situation," is crucial in determining when to read, how to position yourself, and your overall goal for reading a particular book. From the second aspect, the "gold miner mindset" and the "one thing principle" come into play when you annotate the book and choose the most relevant chapter to read that will address the one big question that you seek an answer to. The final aspect, "building your reading habit around your situation, goal, and available cognition," encapsulates the whole process from start to finish.

In pursuit of streamlining your reading habits so that you can quickly and effortlessly ingest the most pressing knowledge, the next chapter tackles common misconceptions about reading.

CHAPTER 3
READING MYTHS

If you know the enemy and know yourself, you need not fear the result of a hundred battles. If you know yourself but not the enemy, for every victory gained you will also suffer a defeat. If you know neither the enemy nor yourself, you will succumb in every battle.

— **Sun Tzu** in *The Art of War*

* * *

MYTH #1:
WHAT BOOK DO YOU RECOMMEND I READ?

A few years ago, I formed a mastermind group of six members. We meet weekly to share our progress and keep each other accountable to our goals. In the same hangout, we also share what we learned the previous week, and it is mandatory for every member to share. If a member doesn't have anything to share, he or she has to read a book and share the new idea.

At one point, we were having a heated discussion about *The Fountainhead*. A few members in the group were sharing how *The Fountainhead* had greatly impacted their thinking. Somehow I got annoyed and got to an argument with them. At that time, I was not a fan of fiction-style teaching. Plus, I was also not convinced that *The Fountainhead* deserved more attention than other personal development books.

As Charlie Munger, a respected investor and a billionaire, said, "I never allow myself to have an opinion on anything that I don't know the other side's argument better than they do," so I decided to read the book *The Fountainhead* myself—to be able to make an informed stance.

I told my team that I would finish the book by our next meeting. Not only that, but I would also read another book about sales, recommended by another member, to show my willingness to learn and so that I could give an objective judgment on which book yielded greater benefit.

Now looking back, I admit it was just a silly act rather than a humble attempt to learn. Even still, I learned a great lesson from the experience. I hadn't realized that that discussion would be the beginning of a long break in my reading journey.

Reading those two books was surprisingly painful. It was the third day I'd spent on *The Fountainhead*, and I was going nowhere. For the previous three days, I'd only managed to read it for one hour each day. No matter how hard I tried, I couldn't digest the book. It was not that the book was bad; something was wrong with me. On the fourth day, I felt a strong force of resistance trying to block me from picking up the book.

I finished the book after ten days—not an enjoyable ten days, as I'd hoped for. Though it was not my normal reading style, I progressed through the book page by page. I was afraid of missing the information that my friend was talking about. I also didn't want to deal with the guilt of missing important details.

The next book on sales was no better. I was not interested in anything other than technology at that time in my life. Reading a book on the topic of sales was like driving on the wrong side of the road.

My patience was at its limit. I ended up stopping halfway through the sales book. Worst of all, not having any guidance on effective reading, I made the mistake of concluding that reading was a waste of time—under any circumstance. There seemed nothing to gain after almost 20 days of dedicated reading. And there followed a long six-month break from reading, which I later regretted.

More often, people start their reading journeys by asking friends, *"What book do you recommend I read?"* It's a dangerous question. Often, people unintentionally give recommendation without knowing much about the asker's true motive.

Perhaps a better question to ask is, "I'm trying to learn about [insert skill here]. What do you recommend I read?" With luck, they might raise the question to the right expert on the subject, who happens to also understand which knowledge is best for a particular entry point, and then rightful guidance could be given.

Even then, that guidance is not often appropriately matched with the reader's unique situation, thus leading to the reader feeling frustrated and losing trust in the knowledge that could be gained from reading the particular book.

Not having any reading activity is unwise. But reading the wrong book is even worse. I would rather not read any book than read the wrong book.

KNOW WHERE YOU ARE FIRST.

Roger Hamilton, a multimillionaire and the author of *The Millionaire Master Plan*, explained that when he was seeking knowledge from books, he was very confused. Each new book's advice seemed to contradict the advice in the book he'd just finished.

With his head spinning, Roger looked into business role models instead. That didn't work out better. From his observation, "Richard Branson wrote that it is all about being the entrepreneur adventure, but then Jack Welch proved you could reach the top working for others. Oprah Winfrey shows the power of shining from the front with the stars while Mark Zuckerberg was happy to hack in the back in his hoodie. Warren Buffet and Bill Gates may make significant bridge partners, but they had entirely different paths to success: Buffet invests in many businesses but never in anything high-tech; Gates focused his life on growing just one high-tech business."

Hamilton then set out on the mission to find not only his path but also the entire map of wealth creation. That was when he discovered a simple but hidden fact: *All of that advice and knowledge are all correct; we are all on the same map—just in different places.* While it is important to know where you want to go, it doesn't matter if you don't know who you are or even where you are.

Different people are at different stages (of wealth creation) and have different strengths, thus different needs. One piece of advice can be a lifesaver for one person but useless for another. Reading books operates the same way. One book can be life-changing for one person but offer nothing to other people in different situations.

Roger Hamilton is on to something. It is critical not only which book you read, but equally so, which book you choose NOT to read. Every time you read the right book, it puts you a little bit ahead of the game. For every wrong book you read, whether wrong type, wrong timing, or wrong order, your reading practice suffers some damage.

Your goal is to read as much of the right ones as possible and to avoid the wrong ones. That way you are getting ahead of the game fast enough to build permanent momentum, before you stack up enough damage and give up on your reading.

The deliberated reading approach addresses differently the myth of casual book recommendations. It applies "selective focus" on the right type of book. The steps to create "selective focus," once followed, will win you back time and protect your reading habit from being lost.

MYTH #2
MASTERING SPEED-READING IS NECESSARY.

There is a story about an Indian businessman who heard about a holy man who could walk on water. The businessman reasoned that if he could walk on water, the publicity would help his business. He decided to seek out the holy man. The holy man agreed to take him on as a disciple.

"All you need to do is follow these meditations, stop eating these foods, and say these prayers. Then you can walk on water like me," the holy man advised.

The businessman smiled with delight. "That's it? Wonderful. I'll start today." He headed for the door.

The holy man cleared his throat. "There is just one more thing. It's a little thing, but very important."

The businessman stood in the doorway impatiently. "Yes?" he asked.

"Don't think about monkeys," the holy man warned.

The businessman looked surprised. "That's easy," he replied and continued heading home.

From that moment, inside the businessman's head, a stream of monkeys appeared: waltzing, dancing, eating, and playing. As he drove home, he pictured every monkey he had ever seen in books. That night, monkeys swung through his dreams. Within a week, he was monkey mad.

The story demonstrates how the human mind is full of mystery and hard to control. If you try to control it, it will play all kinds of tricks on you. Tell it to stop thinking, and a stream of thought will come. Tell it to think of a quiet lake surface, and in it appears all sorts of distortion and noise.

For a quick demonstration, try this: Don't think of a pink elephant for the next five minutes. See if you can do it.

Unlocking brainpower and optimizing it for learning is a dream of many researchers.

There are countless books and research on the potential of the human brain and its application to reading. One such heavily researched and scrutinized technique is speed-reading.

Speed-reading entails optimizing eye vision, stopping internal vocals, scanning, and skimming. By far, training in this area shows positive results, as the method can successfully boost reading speed from 300 words-per-minute (WPM) to 700 WPM, and even up to 1,000+ WPM for longtime speed-reading practitioners.

When the speed goes up, unfortunately, information retention is not improved at the same rate. The following question has been causing headaches for speed-reading practitioners for years: *After speed-reading a text, how much do you remember after a period of time, for instance three weeks?*

Let's be honest, the answer is—NOT MUCH.

One could argue that if you can retain ten percent of a book, reading 10 books at the same rate would make up for the amount of information you don't retain. However, reading doesn't work that way. Time is not the only resource needed for reading. You consume a good amount of willpower, concentration, and logical thinking while you read, and they are not refilled as fast as you can speed-read.

We need to keep in mind that although speed-reading techniques have improved over the last decade, the human mind has not evolved to process such a great level of information.

In fact, millions of pieces of new information from various media are just waiting to be consumed each day. The human brain has no choice but to adapt by developing a filter system, one that filters more than 99% of that information and only keeps the most relevant pieces. It's the system that protects your brain from being overloaded.

Thus, the book you read won't help if it can't get through the filter and be retained in the memory.

Still, people often overrate speed-reading. They get addicted to it. When a person practices speed-reading and sees their WPM increase, their brain releases dopamine that brings short-term comfort. As the person continues to speed-read, they get better and feel more confident—until the point when they start noticing a significant gap between their eyes and brain as they are going through the information.

Most of the time during speed-reading, the brain has to play a catch-up game, which it is terrible at and usually loses.

The observed symptom is to feel sleepy while reading. The larger the gap between the speed of the eyes and the brain, the faster it feels tired.

Eventually, the reader's learning rate plateaus. Occasionally, it even falls freely into a deep dip. From here, there is a high chance that the reader may drop the ball and give up on speed-reading, or even no longer believe in the value of books.

Brain training is meant to enhance reading. Without proper use, it could backfire and leave a negative impact over the long term.

If you are just getting started, don't worry too much about practicing to speed-read. You can slowly learn it along the way. Your speed will naturally increase as you implement the "deliberated reading" approach in this book. Speed-reading is just an optional enhancement.

In the next section, we will learn the last myth that can keep readers from being efficient. By being aware of this simple human fallacy, readers can be free to perform at the levels they expect and choose that are right for them, instead of depending on an author's roadmap.

MYTH #3
YOU BETTER READ THE WHOLE BOOK.

It is easier to resist at the beginning than at the end.

—Leonardo Da Vinci

In his popular book *Influence: The Psychology of Persuasion*, Cialdini talks about the commitment trap he learned from buying toys for his son.

It was January, and he was at the town's largest toy store. After purchasing too many gifts for his son on Christmas, he had sworn not to enter that store again. Yet there he was, not only in the diabolic place but also in the process of buying his son another expensive toy.

The odd thing is that he happened to meet a former neighbor who was buying the same toy. In fact, they had both bought their sons expensive post-Christmas gifts the previous year as well.

Later he discovered that it was not a coincidence. He learned how several of the big toy companies jacked up their January and February sales.

They started prior to Christmas with attractive TV ads for certain special toys. Kids, naturally wanting what they saw, extracted Christmas promises for these items from their parents.

Now here's where the genius of the companies' plans came in: They undersupplied the stores with the toys the parents had promise to get.

Most parents found those toys sold out and were forced to substitute other toys of equal value. The toy manufacturers, of course, made an effort to supply the stores with plenty of these substitutes.

Then, after Christmas, the companies started running the ads again for the original special toys. This juiced up the kids to want those toys more than ever. They went running to their parents, whining, "You promised, you promised," and the adults went trudging off to the store to live up dutifully to their pledge.

In the story, a promise (in another word, a commitment) is the key. "Commitment" means to take a stand or to go on record. **Once an act of commitment is made, there is a natural tendency to behave in ways that are stubbornly consistent with the stand; and it can bias us toward subsequent consistent choices.**

It explains why readers tend to read a book page by page from start to finish after purchasing. Buying a book is an act of commitment, and the buyer feels obligated to read it thoroughly after making the purchasing decision.

The more expensive the book, the more firm the commitment to read it completely. Without understanding commitment bias, people read books from chapter to chapter thinking they read them because the content is good.

It is true that there are good chapters. Unfortunately, it's not all of them. There are good chapters and bad chapters. Some chapters are good *for you*, and some chapters aren't.

Most people read because they purchased the book as a whole. If books were sold in chapter units (instead of entire books), people would quickly learn that there is absolutely no need to read a book from cover to cover. There is no obligation whatsoever. And you need no permission to read the book halfway.

Reading a book from start to finish leads to long hours spent going at it in its entirety, and opportunity cost starts adding up. You can easily verify this phenomenon with these simple questions.

After you read the book, let it settle for one day, then ask: "Knowing what I know now and the amount of key information I retained from the book, how much time do I wish I'd spent reading this book? Which single chapter do I determine to have been the most crucial?" Then, take one more step by answering, "What could I possibly have done with those hours if I hadn't spent them reading the whole book?"

Commonly, you will learn from the answers that not all the chapters in a book matter equally.

A single book typically has one or two key points, covered in one or two chapters. As long as you can grab those points, the book is worth its price.

You should then allow yourself to take back the time and perhaps invest it in another book. You might not notice this, but anytime you consider buying a book, you always have an end goal. It could be to learn a skill or to do some certain task effectively.

Your goal should be the driver of your reading. It should guide you in making the decision about which chapters you read, rather than letting the commitment bias take over, causing you to read the whole book.

But, I read the whole book because I'm a perfectionist.

Jason Fried talks about workaholics in his book, *Rework*, "In the end, workaholics don't actually accomplish more than non-workaholics. They may claim to be perfectionists, but that just means they're wasting their time fixating on inconsequential details instead of moving on to the next task. Workaholics aren't heroes. They don't save the day, they just use it up. The real hero is already home because she figured out a faster way to get things done."

Based on Jason's sentiment, I pose the following question: *In reading a book from start to finish, are you simply wasting time fixating on inconsequential details or are you performing?*

In closing the chapter, we have visited all three myths that commonly result in ineffective reading, something many beginners engage in. Even seasonal readers sometimes fall for these myths. After eliminating ineffective reading behaviors, we will need to replace them with a much more efficient and result-driven approach.

In the next four chapters, we move on to discuss in greater depth "deliberated reading," the much simpler way to read that does not entail speed-reading.

SIDE STORY: THE DARK SIDE OF AUTHORING
In writing this book, I joined a community of authors. We share tips and support each other along the way in our writing. One rule we keep reminding each other is to avoid putting "fluff" into our books. It is boring, and readers don't like it.

Unfortunately, the way book publishing is structured still revolves around word count. An author needs to hit a certain word count threshold for their idea to be considered a "book." Less than a certain number of words, and people doubt if you have the necessary authority to write on a subject.

This word-count requirement creates two sides of a coin. On the one hand, it encourages authors to really dive in and thoroughly develop their book ideas, so that they can reach the required number of words. On the other hand, it creates more opportunity for authors to introduce fluff into their writing.

With the rise of self-publishing, the latter is becoming the norm.

CHAPTER 4
DELIBERATED READING ASPECT #1
SELECTIVE FOCUS

The first component of my deliberated reading approach is **selective focus**. Selective focus is the practice of choosing the right book to read. Selective focus is achieved by being aware of and following two ideas. First, you need to know your strengths, weaknesses, and current situation. Then, you focus all your energy on solving your number one problem by leveraging your strengths.

THE ART OF SELF-MANAGEMENT

Peter Drucker, a master in management, described it perfectly: "Most people think they know what they are good at. They are usually wrong. More often, people know what they are not good at—and even then more people are wrong than right. And yet, a person can perform only from strength. One cannot build performance on weaknesses, let alone on something one cannot do at all."

Do you know what your strengths are? Can your strengths fill in the gap and help you move to the next desired stage?

We learned from myth #1 (about casual book recommendations) that to get to where you want, you need to know where you are first. By understanding your position, you can efficiently map out the easiest and most effortless route to the destination. Only then, you know the gap and pick the right book. The first step in the process is to master the "3 Knows-Knows."

THE 3 KNOW-KNOWS

- **Know Your Strengths:** There are dozens of personality tests you can take online to understand more about yourself. To name a few: the Myers-Briggs Types Indicators (MBTI), Strength Finder, and Visual-Auditory-Kinesthetic learning styles. I would recommend you take all those tests or take as many as you can. You could visit <u>http://effortless-reading.com/resources</u> for links to those tests.

One factor to finding the right book is to understand how much your strengths align with the author's strengths. You may be a practical type of person, who would like to have a plan fully laid out before taking any action. Then, you probably would find it much more comfortable to read a book from an author who also emphasizes strategy and planning. In that case, a screw-it-just-do-it type of book is not the right one for you.

- **Know Your Stage:** What's your current finance stage? Where are you at with your career? Being aware of the context as well as your situation filters out inapplicable books. Authors usually write books for a particular audience in predefined situations. Unfortunately authors frequently do not communicate this clearly because they don't want to lose any readers. Or the reader does not take it seriously when the author discusses their intended audience in the book's foreword.

If you are at a stage of insecure or weak finance, avoid reading a book about thinking big and following your passion. It will backfire and won't solve your problem. Read a book to learn how to achieve high performance, how to motivate yourself to work hard, and how to stabilize your finances. You can't think big when your stomach is empty. When you move to a more stable finance stage, you can start pushing the limit by reading about creativity or thinking big.

Similarly, you should focus on professional and

technical books when you are a junior in a company. Only start learning about teamwork or persuasion after you reach a senior position.

- **Know Your Problem:** People wear different hats during the day. A person could play the role of a dad, a boss, a friend, and a husband in the same day. In one moment, he's a manager at work. In another, he's a dad at home. Every day, people have to deal with different aspects of life, typically including health, wealth, relationships, or happiness. Any of these areas could have ups and downs.

  You might have to deal with both finance and relationship issues at the same time. They usually relate to each other. One area underperforming leads to problems in another area. However, if you pay close attention to your thoughts, you will realize the majority of the time you are thinking about only one problem—the most impactful one and also the most uncomfortable one. It is typically the one that you most procrastinate about, and it scares you the most. Can you identify what it is and how it was formed?

Collecting the 3 Knows-Knows sets you on the successful path. The next step is to aim toward your destination and go at it full speed.

THE ONE THING

I can't stress enough how critical it is to get this practice done right. If it is possible, I would recommend you pick up the book, *The One Thing*, by Gary Keller after finishing this book.

41

He describes it in much more detail and with elegance. I want to offer you his book's essential idea with the following focus question:

(1) *What's the* **one thing** *I can do, (2) such that by doing it, (3) everything else will be easier or unnecessary?*

There are three folds in this focus question to pay attention to. First, notice it asks you to determine the "one thing" that is achievable. Second, there's the criterion that you need to meet "by doing it," rather than just "thinking about it." The last fold gives the game-changing results—this one thing has so much impact that it could change "everything" to "easier or unnecessary."

It is an extremely powerful approach to living your life. Basically, you boost one area so ridiculously high that it could outweigh and rewrite the meaning of all other things.

Charlie Munger, the famous billionaire, also agrees with this, "In business we often find that the winning system goes almost ridiculously far in maximizing or minimizing one or a few variables."

The principle operates the same way in choosing the book to read.

Once you have executed the first part of selective focus, you should know what is that "one thing" you need to take on. If done right, you are not only aware of that one thing, but you also understand well the context around it and whether you have the necessary skills to get it done. This becomes the criteria to choose your next book.

The next books you read need to address, at least 80%, this issue. If you need to find a job, the next 4 out of 5 books you buy need to be about job finding, writing resumes, interviewing, or an optional book on body language. If health is your problem, you need to double up on reading books on diet, eating, and nutrition.

Solve your number one problem first.

CHAPTER 5
DELIBERATED READING ASPECT #2
REPETITION

You are the average of the five people you spend the most time with.

—**Jim Rohn**

* * *

I observe this "average five" phenomenon in myself. As I move up my career ladder, I hang out with new friends all the time.

My new friends usually share my same wealth level. Some friends are doing better, some are a little bit behind, but in general, we look at life with the same lens. On average, I make about 20 new friends every year. However, only a few of those friends have a significant impact on me. They are the people I spend most of my time with.

When I first heard about the "average five" principle, I was in awe. In response, I reduced contacts with those who were significantly less successful than I was and started using that additional time to hang out with those who had achieved more than I had.

That simple act immediately changed my life. I have more

energy and excitement being around highly successful people. Their attitudes towards problems and their speed of executing solutions inspire me. What I have learned is to make sure I carefully choose whom I want to spend time with.

Books operate the same way. Charlie "Tremendous" Jones said, "Five years from today, you will be the same person that you are today, except for the books you read and the people you meet."

The books you read have as much impact on your life as your closest friends. As you have many friends, you can read many books, but be picky about which ones you will allow to be in your inner circle. Choosing the right one lifts you up, and the bad one pulls you down.

Don't be afraid to stop reading a book that you don't feel strongly about and start spending more time reading repeatedly the best books you have. I read my 150 best books of all times repeatedly, to the point I remember almost everything from the books.

I'd rather have four quarters than one hundred pennies.

Although a cliché, it's an interesting analogy. Visualize carrying one hundred pennies in your pocket: They're noisy, uncomfortable, and all-around inconvenient. It's difficult to keep track of all of them. And, let's be honest, if you were to drop one, would you bother to pick it up?

Now imagine carrying four quarters. Compared to the one

hundred pennies, they're light, easy to find, and, most importantly, they have worth. If you drop one, you're going to pick it up, not because it's worth twenty-five pennies (although it is), but because you have only three left.

Cheesy, sure. But it proves the point: Why carry one hundred just for the sake of friendship itself when you have the ability to devote twenty-five times more attention to a smaller number of people? It isn't the friendship itself that brings us joy and contentment; it's what we take from (and give to) it.

[A post of I.M.H.O Medium.com account]

The second component of deliberated reading is not volume, but repetition.

If you have the mindset of reading a book just once, then you will be worried if you missed one idea from the book. But think about how you meet your friends for the first time—you might find some spark, but you don't try to find out everything about the person in the initial encounter.

Making a friend is a process. It takes many rounds and events to get to know one person thoroughly. The same thinking should be applied to reading. By having multiple passes, you get to know the book's concepts and learn how the author structures ideas and puts them together. Between passes, you have a chance to implement the book's idea and check what's working and what's not. Then you can incorporate that feedback into the next pass.

This approach has been proven many times in the intellectual industry. Eric Rise describes a similar approach in his book *Lean Startup*. In a startup, a group of visionary people get together to build a minimal viable product (MVP) and ship it to the market for feedback. Using that feedback, they further enhance the product and ship it to the market again.

The core idea is that you should not waste time building a full-fledged product at the beginning without knowing what works and what doesn't. With the complexity of the market, trying to create a complete product is risky and costly.

When you read a new book with a new concept, you probably don't have much idea how to implement them. You also don't know the author enough to understand his or her motivations or messages.

Reading a book in one full pass and trying to apply all its concepts has the same level of risk as releasing a full-fledged product in one shot. The recommended way is to go through it in multiple passes, starting with learning the most important concepts and then expanding to more details in future re-readings.

Repetition forms a deep relationship between you and the book. Only then, it can start casting its effects into your daily life. Biologically speaking, reading contributes to the brain's ability to connect and integrate various sources of information—especially, visual with auditory, linguistic, and conceptual areas. The speed of that integration depends a great deal on the myelination of neutrons' axons.

Simply put, as you read, the layers of myelin around axons get thicker. Thick layers allow information to flow faster. As a result, your decisions and judgments (which happen in just a few milliseconds) could be backed by more information.

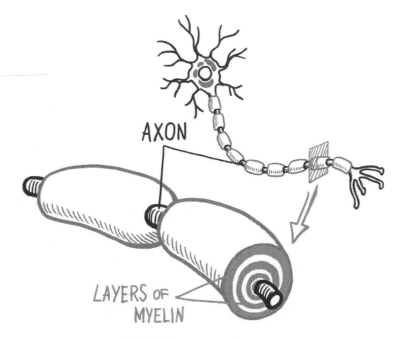

AXON

LAYERS OF MYELIN

Myelin layers around an axon

ADDING THE REPETITION FACTOR TO READING

To start coordinating repetition into your reading, keep a list of the best 50 to 150 books that you will return to and reread every year.

If you have less than 50, it does not cover enough breadth. If you have more than 150, you start losing track of the essentials and will have a difficult time revisiting them.

The original science of 150 is based on what we know about the human mind. Dr. Robin Dunbar, a famous social scientist, uncovered in his research that the human mind can maintain up to 150 relationships in optimal settings.

Dunbar's number represents the cognitive limit to the number of people with whom one can maintain stable social relationships. To be included in this number, which is theoretically ~150, the person must know who each individual is and how each is connected to others within the social web.

Over time, your situations, focus, and interests in life might change. After a few rounds of reading the same book, a few concepts might no longer be useful to you. Allow yourself to remove it from the list or replace the book with a better one. Repeat the process until the point you can proudly introduce those books to your peers—those at your level, or even your mentors or managers.

Keep in mind that it doesn't mean you should only read 150 books. Rather, you should schedule your reading to balance between reading new books and rereading those 150.

Rereading takes less time, and you often learn more by rereading. The first pass though a book is full of excitement, as your brain loves learning new things. The second pass, however, is often the most useful. It gives you a chance to evaluate how you have applied an idea and to correct a few details to make it better.

Here are a few tools to help track those books. Some of them are more convenient than others, so choose the one that best fits your style:

1. Offline Document: The simplest way to keep track of your books is to create a document on your computer and start recording the list of books, plus authors' names. You can use Microsoft Word, or any note-taking application you have on your computer. Pen and paper work too—you just need to ensure you know where to find your list.

2. Online Document: You can use Google Docs, or online notes like Evernote (evernote.com) or Microsoft OneNote to save the list as well. The advantage of the online document is that you have access to it everywhere.

3. Book Platform Service: Many book community platforms help track the books you read. GoodReads (Goodreads.com), Booklikes.com, Shefari.com, LibraryThing.com, and Google Books are the most popular ones. They all come with great features allowing you to interact with friends and authors, and to write reviews, notes, and much more.

Many of these platform don't allow you to create a separated list for your top 150 books. You could work around by using their rating system to mark the top 150 instead.

Even if you choose not to use those platform services, try to maintain two lists of books: a list of books you have read and a list that you wish to read. In the first list, mark your top 150. By tracking the number of books and your top ones, it gives you motivation to keep engaging and reading. As the list grows, you can use it to reflect on the amount of knowledge you have been ingesting.

So far, we have learned how to choose books with **selective focus** and how to "make friends" with books by practicing **repetition**. Those steps together ensure your reading is focused and meaningful. In the next section, we will explore how to build a strong foundation for reading that guarantees your personal growth both in the short and long terms.

CHAPTER 6
DELIBERATED READING ASPECT #3
BALANCE

You cannot build a dream on a foundation of sand. To weather the test of storms, it must be cemented in the heart with uncompromising conviction.

—T.F. Hodge

* * *

To illustrate the third element of deliberate reading, let's examine two popular books of our time, *The 4-Hour Workweek* by Tim Ferris and *Think and Grow Rich* by Napoleon Hill. They are books that brought the authors to the spotlight and made their names quite well-known.

Each book's content is superb as well. *The 4-Hour Workweek* (*4HWW*) comprises a list of techniques to optimize your performance at work, such as reducing emails, reading news, outsourcing your job, setting up automatic systems, and so on. *Think and Grow Rich* captures 13 success principles from 500 wealthy people that Hill spent 20 years interviewing and studying.

Even with their excellent content followed by great stories, most readers fail to take action after finishing the books. The first time I read *4HWW*, I felt inspired but overwhelmed with its many technical details and tactics. Some of them were already out of date (I read *4HWW* four years after it was published) or not applicable to my situation.

On the other hand, Hill's book weighed heavier on the opposite side. It focuses on the principles and mindsets to achieve the goals. They are the foundation blocks that you can build your skills on. The downside is that Hill does not offer any concrete actions to take or tell you exactly where to start.

Those two books represent two buddies of yours, "tactics" and "philosophy." They are good friends, and you need both of them to achieve meaningful results. They operate like two children on a seesaw. As one pulls down, the other is pushed up. As you read books about tactics, you need to ensure you spend time on upgrading your philosophy to match the tactics level as well.

They both need their share of your time. If you weigh heavily on one end and stay there for too long, the other end gets hurts and is not happy. The seesaw is fun if only there is motion coming from both sides.

Are you keeping your seesaw in motion?

Deliberate Reading Works When the Balance Is in Motion.

More often, people do not know that reading must keep up with the multiple latitudes of life. This overlooked truth is why most beginner readers find reading not as applicable as they expect and gradually give up on it.

To build solid knowledge from reading, it is critical that you master both the technique and the philosophy. My mentor, Tai Lopez, recommends distributing your reading among the following categories: classics, how-to, "tactics" books, and autobiographies and biographies.

1. Classic Books: Classics are the books that have passed the test of time—books that last for 20 years. And even better if they have been around more than 50 years. Their authors are often the great thinkers of the century. Hence, the content is usually well researched and validated. In practice, the classics' principles should be applicable for many decades.

These books help sharpen your own philosophy, offering the foundation blocks to build other tactical skills.

Some good examples include Peter Drucker's various books on business, Napoleon Hill's *Think and Grow Rich*, Dale Carnegie's *How to Win Friends and Influence People*, and writing by Seneca, Aristotle, or Karl Marx.

2. How-To or "Tactics" Books: These are books that go straight to the point, laying out all the information in an easy-to-consume format. These books often have "How To" or

"Practice" in their titles. These are the books that you walk away from with something tangible, either a skill or steps to perform certain tasks.

Generally, they provide up-to-date knowledge. On the other hand, these books have short life-spans. In fact, you will need to pay close attention to the book's publishing date before purchasing. Make sure it is not too far off from the present. Different industries have different turnover times for their books. Technology books change very quickly. It takes about 18 months for a particular technology to either evolve or be discarded. Other categories, like health or studying methods, have not changed much in the last decades.

Good examples of "tactics" books include Guy Kawasaki's *The Art of Start*, Richard Koch's *The All-Day Energy Diet* and *The 80/20 Principle*, and Robert Kiyosaki's *Rich Dad Poor Dad*.

3. Autobiographies and Biographies: These include the stories of the lives of our world's famous people. Autobiographies and biographies are not quick reads, but rather offer the significant challenges these people were facing while making their way into the high-impact-people club. Not only do you learn how to obtain a particular skill set, but studying their stories also equips you with great lessons you can't find anywhere else.

Autobiographies and biographies enlarge your vision beyond your current situation. You can see ahead, what to expect, and what to avoid. The books highlight the primary events, which you might encounter if you are on a similar path.

Some achievements could easily cost the smartest person ten to twenty years to reach. But if you ask those people, they will likely tell you most of that time was wasted. They could have made more correct decisions with effective use of resources if they have had the vision they currently have. And through an autobiography or biography that ready-made vision is offered for your taking.

Another powerful aspect of this genre is that in reading autobiographies and biographies, the courage of the subject extends to your daily activities. Courage is the one of the most important elements that you need in order to succeed.

In your life, you will need to have courage, and you will need lots of it. Learning of the courageous decisions of influential people gets you familiar with pivotal life decisions. When it's your turn, you can make a impactful call.

By seeing other extraordinary people handle fear and accomplish the same thing that you are trying to do, you will be able to build up your courage and inspiration to do the same.

Some powerful examples of autobiographies and biographies include Sir Richard Branson's *Screw It, Let's Do It*, Arnold Schwarzenegger's *Total Recall*, Sam Walton's *Made in America*, and Jerry Weintraub's *When I Stop Talking, You'll Know I'm Dead*. The biographies of Steve Jobs, the Dalai Lama, and Mother Teresa are valuable as well.

Most books in the three categories tend to share different aspects. Some may give stories, discuss only a few principles, and mostly focus on tactics. Others may only have stories and draw on principles from the stories, without suggesting any concrete, actionable items.

As you choose which book to read, try to distribute evenly among the three types.

Though, there will be a time in your life that you need to skew towards one category more than the others. If you are dealing with insecure finances, then focus on the how-to and tactics group. If you have a job and are efficient at work, read the classics to understand your next jump. At some point, you will be confronting life-changing events. Learning about people who have achieved similar things will supply the vision and courage you may need.

Still, it's important to keep your focus balanced and always in motion—just like the seesaw.

By understanding the purpose of the three types, your reading will benefit from being balanced between tactics, philosophy, and modeling. Your reading will become much more effortless simply by choosing the right type of book.

In the next chapter, we will discuss how to determine your optimal settings and perspectives while reading those three kinds of book, in order to learn how to align them with the natural development of the human brain.

SIDE STORY: DEFUSE YOUR MIND FOR A GOOD NIGHT'S SLEEP

Tim Ferris, the author of *The 4-Hour Workweek*, reads fiction as a way to defuse his mind away from being productive and pragmatic (left brain) before bed. By switching to a relaxed state, your sleep can come to you more easily and get deeper. Autobiographies and biographies could offer a similar effect.

CHAPTER 7
DELIBERATED READING ASPECT #4
GETTING IN THE RIGHT GEAR

Have you ever tried to speed-read a book, but it was so dense that you ended up not taking anything away? Was there a moment you completely understood every word but had a hard time making sense of the paragraph as a whole?

On those occasions, most likely you needed to shift your reading gear. Getting into the right gear puts you, the reader, into the optimal setting to consume the material effortlessly. It helps avoid brain crashes and unexpected incidents. Getting into this right gear is an essential step in building a sustainable reading habit. To better understand the reading gear, think of how a person drives on the road.

WHAT IS A READING GEAR?
Reading, in many ways, resembles driving on the road.

In driving, the speed limit in cities is often about 20–25 miles per hour (MPH) and about 50–80 MPH on highway. You have to slow down in cities because the roads are narrower. There are many intersections, pedestrians, and complicated road rules applied when you navigate your way through the city. In other words, the "density" of the city enforces drivers to pay more attention and drive very carefully.

On the highway, driving becomes much simpler. Everyone moves in the same direction. The roads are bigger. There are fewer distractions and surprises. As a result, you can speed up and drive for hours on the highway effortlessly.

For these reasons, you learn not to speed in the cities because it's dangerous. You also learn that driving slowly on the highway is as dangerous as racing in the cities.

Reading operates in the same way. It is harmful to use the same reading speed to handle different types of books. In reading, "crashes" happen when your reading speed does not align with the type of book you're reading. The symptoms of a reading crash include feeling sleepy after a short time, the inability to retain or to link together the information, getting lost in the big picture, or diving too deeply into the story without learning any lesson.

To avoid such brain crashes, you need to take into account the type and density of the book. Different types of books demand different "gears" and speeds. We talked about the three types of books in the previous chapter—classics, how-to, "tactics" books, and autobiographies and biographies. Being aware of and applying the right gear for the right type of book helps keep you safe on the reading trip. Let's start with the easiest, the how-to, "tactics" book.

THE HOW-TO, "TACTICS" BOOK – GEAR 3 – LIGHT WILLPOWER REQUIRED

A how-to, "tactics" book entails the easiest type of reading. It's like driving on the highway. You should be able to read it at the fastest speed possible. You can speed up your reading as long as you can still understand the chapter's main point. These books are straightforward and easy to digest. Some of them follow a "hand-holding" style, meaning you can follow it step by step and achieve the desired result with few to no surprises.

How-to, "tactics" books are the types in which you can find high recurrences of the same central ideas. The main ideas might be introduced to you through different stories, but the messages are the same. Their chapters are usually well structured, starting with a story (or example), then the thesis, next the application, and finally an exercise model. If you are familiar with the subject, feel free to skip the story, glance through the thesis, and spend more time on the application section.

The book, *The Success Principles*, by Jack Canfield is a typical example. In it the author collected short stories and turned them into principles. If you love reading fiction, you will find this book entertaining. It doesn't require lots of thinking, and you can read at anytime of the day.

Here's the key: A single tactics book will only have one or two points applicable to you at the time of reading. The rest is either example stories, insignificant points, or just not applicable at the moment to you. Your brain, at the reading time, doesn't have enough context to sculpt all the points of a book into its long-term memory. You cannot cook a dish without all the ingredients (the context), so just chill, and come back to it at a later time when you have the need for more information.

Generally, you should speed up your reading straight to where the main message is, then slow down around that specific chapter, and finally speed up through the rest.

THE CLASSIC BOOK – GEAR 2 – HIGH WILLPOWER REQUIRED

The classic books should be read more slowly than the how-to, "tactics" books. **Classics are designed to be read at a moderate pace.** The teachings in classics have been proven over and over in the last decades (or maybe even the last centuries). They demand more attention. You should allow more time to understand them and to reflect upon your own experience while reading them.

The time it took the author to write a classic book is generally much longer than the content of the book itself. As Brian Tracy noted, the author needs to know ten words in order to write a word in a book. For classics, it could go up to 100 words for every word written.

It took Napoleon Hill more than 20 years to write *Think and Grow Rich*. Will Durant spent decades learning about history before writing *The Lessons of History*. They are all smart people. It is obvious that you can't absorb years of experience within a few hours.

Some classic books also require preparation, like understanding the age of the year it was published and the major events of that age. Books written in the Renaissance or the time of a world war likely have tones and language different from the modern world.

By reading the book jacket, the purpose of the book, about the time it was published, and the "about the author" section, you will find it easier to digest a classic book and understand why it was written that way and how much of the book is still applicable in the current world.

As a result of your formulating the context and your filtering process, your reading speed will slow down. However, once you can read the book with the lens of history (context) on, you are set to reach a higher level of reading comprehension.

Different from how-to, "tactics" books, classics often contain more than one gold nugget, typically around 5–10. Sometimes they compliment each other and form a "framework," so it is necessary to go both broad and deep here.

To give an example, *The Seven Habits of Highly Successful People* by Stephen Covey covers three individual and four team habits, in which each group of habits supports the others. By learning all of the basic concepts, it helps you understand the essentials of one habit in a system and motivates you to build the habit into your daily life.

For the first book pass, I would recommend familiarizing yourself with at least a one-sentence description of all the fundamental principles in the book. Then pick (only) ONE of the principles to dive deeply into. It is totally fine if you pick the wrong one. You can always go back to the others later.

Since classic type requires a certain amount of will power, it is best to read a classic early in the morning, before or after breakfast, when you are fresh and energized after a good night's sleep.

THE AUTOBIOGRAPHY OR BIOGRAPHY – GEAR 1 – EASY RIDING

This type of book is to be read in the lowest gear. You need to understand your end game goal while reading an autobiography or biography. The moment you understand how you want to project yourself into their (the author's) life, then you will stop bouncing back and forth and start catching the book's core stories.

Autobiographies and biographies typically share a similar tone as fiction books—highly entertaining and engaging. And the learning is embedded in the sequences of stories, making it a pleasurable experience to digest.

Unless you know the subject of the autobiography or biography and his or her life story inside out, it's not recommended to jump ahead and skip a few chapters. When I first learned about Arnold Schwarzenegger as a governor, I was not familiar with his name or his career. Only through his autobiography, *Total Recall*, did I learn how he went to America and built his career up from the bottom. I started to understand why people respect him for what he has been doing.

As always, the "heroic" scene was buried somewhere in the book. Depending on where you are in your life, you might have more interest in the starter phase (the discovery phase) or the heroic one (when the subject takes bold actions and conquers the greatest challenges).

Keep in mind that the goal of reading an autobiography or biography is to immerse yourself in the subject's life to extend your vision and comfort zone beyond your current circumstances.

As a result, you shall find your own uncertainty regarding an upcoming challenge reduced as your courage increases. Reading of the rewards as well as the regret of not taking action upfront through the subject's own story helps you make better decisions and to bypass the fear of failure.

To achieve all of these effects, your pace of reading needs to be moderate, so that your brain can replay the major events (usually within a chapter). For each of those events, your goal is to understand:

- The context or situation that the subject was in
- The surrounding human factors, especially the subject's relationships with those around him or her
- The strengths and limitations of the subject at that time, including his or her knowledge, finances, physical being, and mental state

By relating scenarios of the subject's life to your life, you will find courage to take action to reach the hoped-for results.

A unique aspect of the human mind is its capability of simulating an individual's own past experiences (or even those of other people), repeating or reliving that history (do you notice how kids fantasize after watching fairy tale movies?). By feeding a virtual "history" to your brain, it will trigger hormone creation, producing necessary dopamine to drive a particular action. In other words, it will grant you quick access to higher levels of possibility.

Roger Bannister's 4-minute mile run is the classic example. In 1954, he broke the misguided, but common belief that it was impossible for the human body to run one mile within 4 minutes, a belief which held true for years—until Roger broke it. The amazing thing is that barely a year after Roger's historic run, more runners emerged who achieved the same thing. Nowadays, even strong high-school athletes can run a 4-minute mile.

CONTROL YOUR GEAR

The recommended reading paces in this chapter should be used as initial guidance rather than highly strict guidelines in your reading. At any point of reading, you are in full control of your gear. As you build up your domain knowledge, you should allow yourself to change to a higher gear to align well with a topic. Similarly, allow yourself to slow down on a how-to, "tactics" book if it is introducing a new and complicated concept.

As a driver pays attention to the road and drives in the right gear, the car can move for a long time. To sustain reading, you want to do the same, so be picky about the book and choose the appropriate speed to handle the particular type of book you are reading.

Selective focus, **repetition**, **balance**, and **speed** are the four components that make up deliberated reading. Review them frequently in your multiple passes through this book—and apply them always, no matter what text you are reading.

With these four components in action, you will read more quickly, ingest even greater amounts of information, and stay on top of the ever-increasing fount of knowledge in our world today (and in the future...).

The following two chapters will provide you with handy tools to ease your management of that knowledge. Without these tools, your knowledge may become scattered and too weak to deliver the desired results.

CHAPTER 8
READING ROUTINE

We are what we repeatedly do. Excellence, then, is not an act, but a habit.

—Aristotle

* * *

Reading is considerably one of the hardest habits to form, even though the reward is outstanding. Just do a quick search, and you will find tons of blog posts and articles talking about the benefits of reading and how to form a reading habit. It's such a hot topic because of its famously high failure rate. However, those who get it right will be rewarded abundantly.

Though it can take years to form the habit, it only takes a few days to break the chain and lose it. When life demands your attention, reading tends to be at the mercy of other, more pressing tasks.

Putting reading at the bottom of the list is a way of sabotaging your progress. Reading acts like a pump that delivers action and wisdom into your life. When life is overwhelming, you should make sure the plumbing stream is fluent and strong, rather than turning it off. Every time I forget and turn it off, bad things happen. Last time I lost a few grand and six months' worth of work because I didn't continue to read and update my knowledge to match demand.

Now that I understood better how reading should be conducted, it's easier to maintain a routine. As I put down and pick up books many times, it is getting easier with the support of a few key routines. There are many out there, but only a handful work consistently.

KEYS TO DEVELOPING A SUCCESSFUL READING ROUTINE

1. Determine the amount of time you can devote to reading.
Start small—only 10 minutes every day. I'd rather you commit to small amounts of time and hit it every day for an extended period than try to allocate a big block of time, but only last a few days. After each reading, you need to give yourself time to put that knowledge into use.

There are three times in the day you can most benefit from reading. Let's say your reading time lasts 5 minutes per sitting—then you should spend 5 minutes before breakfast, 5 minutes before a nap, and 5 minutes after dinner (or before bed) to read.

Accordingly, classic books are best read in the morning. How-to, "tactics" books can fit in the afternoon before a nap. At the end of the day, reading an autobiography or biography is the best way to help you fall asleep. It can calm you down and detach you from your thoughts of work.

At a minimum, start with 10–15 minutes a day, and do not exceed 45 minutes. It's like lifting weights—it is dangerous to lift too much weight at the beginning. As you get used to reading, you can start to invest more time into it. Ensure you always time your reading. Reading should be a daily activity, not a one-day burst.

2. Set a goal, and plan your reading.

Anything that gets planned, gets done. The reading habit can be formed and improved only if it is quantified and measurable.

Write down your reading goals for the year, divide it into monthly goals, and also plan your reading for each week. The simple act of writing will turn on the commitment bias and help pull you towards actually doing it.

For this year, how many new books are you going to read? Entrepreneurs read on average 50 new books per year (about one book per week), and avid readers read about three books per week. And, even more important, how many books will you be RE-READING this year? Do the same for each month.

Make sure your goal is to have a good mix of new books and the top books you want to reread every year. Rereading a book is equally important as reading a new book. The second and the third passes through a book won't give you the excitement (dopamine) like you get in reading a new book. However, you often learn more because you have done your homework, already having implemented some of the book's advice, so this time you read with experience and context.

If you are not a big fan of planning, you could simply maintain a to-read book list. My queue is a combination of a book wish list—new book names I collected here and there mingled with my top 150 books to reread. Planning is simple—I just take the top books in the queue and read on.

3. Track your progress, and curate your master knowledge list.

Aside from the list of books to be read, you should maintain three other lists:

- A list of books you have read, including titles and authors' names. If you read a book multiple times, record it in multiple entries in this list.

- A list of your favorite books, ranking them in order of importance. I have my top 150 continuously being revised and reordered.

- A list of subjects, including what you have learned, significant quotations, and book names related to subjects. My list includes the following subjects: strength-finding, humility, courage, time management, and more. They are the "cluster of knowledge" that I often refer to when it's time to apply them.

Goodreads, Shelfari, and LibraryThing are platforms that help maintain your reading list as well as social connections around reading. They do not allow you to keep track of the first list I've suggested (book passes) or book rankings (at least at the time of my writing this book). So I usually keep those lists on Evernote. However you choose to keep the lists, be careful as they could get lost over the years.

CHAPTER 9
ANNOTATION CODE

Imagine you are at the cocktail party when someone approaches you with a question, "Would you prefer to work 60 hours a week to earn more money or have a work-life balance instead?" What would be your response?

Can you, without any pause or preparation, deliver a 60-second response and still be persuasive?

We all have those moments. It's the seconds when we wish we could remember and speak confidently about what we have learned and what we believe. Unfortunately, most of the time our minds just turn blank or have difficulty combining ideas together into a convincing speech.

You might have read many books and have tons of ideas, but if you still find yourself in this situation sometimes, there is an easy trick that could instantly help.

Here's a little secret: Successful people compile and maintain their master list of topics and principles. As soon as someone touches on one of those principles, they get excited and could spend a whole evening talking. Tim Ferris is big on meditation and the morning routine. Bill Gates is about working hard. Jeff Bezos values long-term investment. Tai Lopez has 67 principles that he teaches and lives his own life around. The list could go on.

If you haven't started your list, you need to start putting it together.

How Do You Build Your List?

During your reading, there are a few tools to track and organize ideas. For a physical book, the most common two tools are the highlighter and the annotation code. Often, those tools are underutilized for this task. As a deliberate reader, you want to master these tools to ensure your reading is organized, so you minimize wasting resources due to losing track of your thought.

Remember when you were in high school doing some research, you (or your good friend) had a bunch of highlighters and your books were full of color? Since we were kids, many of us were taught to use color-coding to categorize different elements and components in our reading.

I still sometimes use the highlighter method, and I like it a lot. There is nothing that makes the content more outstanding. As I invest more heavily in reading, highlighters, unfortunately, come short in two senses:

- Highlighting is too slow—when I have to highlight multiple lines, it starts to interrupt my reading flow.
- To use more than one color, I have to carry, 3 or 4 highlighters at the same time. I'm then swapping them continuously as I'm highlighting different components. When I'm reading outside my home, the reading session is ruined if I forget my one or all the highlighters.

I recommend using an annotation code over a highlighter. It is quite quick to annotate a paragraph and give it a code, especially in comparison with highlighting. And any pen or pencil is sufficient for this task.

A GOOD ANNOTATION CODE SYSTEM

Aman Anand, an author of multiple novels, shared his annotation code system that he used when researching how to comprehend reading better:

"I = **Idea** derived from what I am reading. For example, while reading a section about a horrible arachnid in *Infinite Jest*, I came up with the idea to have the opening scene of my new book take place on a rooftop garden. The ideas are very much disconnected, but I'll often find some of my best ideas come up while I am reading fiction.

K.Q. = **Key quote.** This note will later be typed up into a list of master quotes, which are then organized by theme, which I will reread once in a while.

P = **Plot.** Crucial points in the plot. These come in particularly useful when I'm trying to remember the precise details of the plot.

S = **Style.** Sentences and passages that are indicative of that writer's particular style."

Timothy Kenny, the author of *Accelerated Learning for Entrepreneurs*, also shared his annotation code system:

Symbols for Reading

(A) Take <u>Action</u> on this

(B) <u>Book</u> to read

(P) <u>Person</u> to learn more about

Q <u>Quote</u>

? I don't understand

✦✦✦ 3 <u>star</u> rating system
✦ important
✦✦ really important
✦✦✦ life changing

Michael Hyatt, the author of multiple best-selling books, uses a similar system to collect information for his speaking and writing. He calls it "note-taking symbols." In his words:

- If an item is particularly important and insightful, I put a star next to it.
- If an item requires further research or resolution, I put a question mark next to it.
- If an item requires follow-up, I put a ballot box (open square) next to it. When the item is completed, I check it off.
- If I have assigned a follow-up item to someone, I put an open circle next to it (similar to the ballot box but a circle rather than square). In the notes, I indicate who is responsible. When the item is completed, I check it off.

And he shares his secret: He scans his notes immediately after the reading if possible. If that is not possible, he will do it at the end of the workday. This way he ensures that he's taking action on those notes.

HOW ABOUT E-BOOK ANNOTATING?

If you are reading mostly e-books, you could annotate by using comments in a hashtag style. Simply highlight the quote you want to note, put a comment with the annotation code within the hashtag or square bracket like this: #q (quote), #a (action), or [q] (quote), [a] action.

GETTING STARTED USING AN ANNOTATION CODE

If you are just getting started with reading, trying to apply a complicated annotation system at the same time could be overwhelming. While it looks easy to use, lots of people fail because pausing to annotate sometimes interrupts their reading flow. Also people easily get uncomfortable if they misuse one of their codes.

A better approach is to take baby steps, learn to use one code at a time. Start with a star rating system first. Keep it simple— at the end of each reading, record all the two-star and three-star sentences in your master quote list. After reading five books, you can start to incorporate more coding into your reading.

To ensure the annotation fits your style, don't hesitate to test various systems. Spend one week working with a particular system to check if it works. If it doesn't, discard it and move on to the next one. Some annotation codes may work for one person but not perform for others. So test it first before you make it your annotation system.

CHAPTER 10
THE FUTURE OF BOOKS

The way we learn has changed over time together with the evolution of materials. Before paper, books were very rare, and even after the advent of the printing press, books were still quite rare. Common people didn't own them. Only the elite and scholars had access to written information and only in the cities where books were located. That knowledge contained in books was so rare that scholar and students learned the books by heart.

When humans invented paper, it revolutionized reading, writing, and the cost of producing information. Books became somewhat more common and accessible to wider audiences. Still, they were limited to where the book was located or delivered.

When the Internet was introduced, it opened a new era of information, creating what we call "global knowledge." Anyone with an Internet connection has access to so much information. Nowadays, books and self-publishing allow people to spread knowledge even faster and more easily.

Knowledge is power. Having quick and efficient access to a source of knowledge gives people advantages over those who don't. There are readers, who are not being exposed to the great book genres. With a limited number of books to read, these readers fall behind important trends. However, readers who can leverage the latest services on the Internet can enhance their learning, cut off years of trial and error, and get ahead of others.

As a humble learner, you want to stay on top of current trends. By understanding how knowledge is spread and the latest convenient ways to accumulate knowledge, you will start getting ahead of the game. A key to staying on top is employing the deliberate reading approach that I've described in this book.

GLOBAL KNOWLEDGE IS ABOUT TO CHANGE MASSIVELY

The most dramatic change in our global knowledge is about to occur between 2016 and 2020. Three to five billion learners, people who have never created or consumed any digital information, are about to go online and provide a mega-surge to the available global knowledge.

While the Internet has been extraordinary, only until recently has it connected the wealthiest. In 2010, 1.8 billion people were connected and had access to digital materials. In 2015, about 2.8 billion have been connected. But in 2020, we expect the **entire world** will be connected, meaning, more than 7 billion people will get online, to learn, observe information, and create new content. There are four major efforts, deploying tens of billions of dollars to make this future happen:

- **Facebook and Internet.org**: They are attempting to design unmanned aircraft that can beam Internet access down to people from the sky.

- **SpaceX Global Constellation**: They propose a project that would use approximately 700 small satellites to provide Internet access to the entire planet, with a strong focus on rural and developing areas.
- **Google Project Loon**: This is a network of thousands of balloons traveling on the edge of space, designed to connect people in rural and remote areas, to help fill coverage gaps and bring people back online after disasters.
- **One Web—Virgin Group & Qualcomm**: They aim to build a satellite network design calling for 650 satellites weighing 125 kg each. Each is capable of delivering at least 8 gigabits per second of throughput to provide Internet access to homes and mobile platforms.

The implication of 7+ billion connected minds is staggering. It represents an addition of at least three times more information and content to global knowledge. What it means is that the learner needs a much better way to navigate in this new world of rich information networks, to grab the most relevant and useful information for their needs. Otherwise, they will get lost in such a large amount of available information. Using the deliberate reading approach I've walked you through in this book will ensure you find yourself successful in the coming data-rich world.

THE CHAPTER BECOMES THE NEW READING UNIT
Accommodating the new wave of information, a new trend is about to happen. Books are getting shorter. The chapter will become the reading unit, which is yet another reason that it is

most efficient to follow the deliberate reading method outlined in this book. Additionally, you should be aware that artificial intelligence (AI) systems are being built to curate personalized knowledge from these chapter pools to best accommodate each reader.

College students should find this approach familiar. Currently, to write a thesis or report, they have to curate information from multiple sources, mostly from the Internet, books, and references from other people. Then, they cross reference the information from those sources to elaborate on a certain point. Their goal is to accumulate knowledge that is well established and examined from different perspectives. This approach is a great way to turn particular knowledge into your instinctual assets.

If it works so well, then why don't people apply the same technique as a daily practice to gain common knowledge? The problem is—**it takes too much time, and it does not scale well**. It takes too much time for an individual to navigate through all the sources and to filter out irrelevant information, which could be better used to dive more deeply into a subject.

Libraries are the pioneers in solving this problem. They employ passionate librarians who can help you find the resources and references you want. But, with the rising rate of content and information coming in the next few years, this manual solution won't scale accordingly. People will need more robust and personalized assistance to help with ingesting new knowledge on a day-to-day basis.

PERSONALIZED READING GETS BETTER

Imagine you have a virtual personal assistant (VPA). Anytime you give it a topic (e.g., low carb diets), in an instant, it connects to the "knowledge mother system" and returns to you with the most relevant information. That information is organized into chapters, from easy to complex.

The magic lies in the accuracy of the content it retrieved for you. It is 100% customized just for you, matching with your personal strengths, as if it were put together by a mentor who has been working closely with you for 5 years and understands what you are good at or capable of.

In order to build such high-quality personal content, the VPA needs to first find hundreds people who share most of your characteristics, such as age, sex, level of education, strengths, learning style, language, culture, and so on.

Among those hundreds people, it then identifies who already knows what you want to know or who has achieved what you desire (e.g., low carb diets). From there, it narrows down the list to about 50 people. Last, it traces back the method and information that those 50 people used to learn about low carb diets, finds the common practical methods, and aggregates them into a "curriculum" for you to follow. Hence, the learning content gets highly personalized, targeted, and equipped with a great success rate.

With big data, artificial intelligence, and the amount of personal data on the web, this future is near. New trends will occur to help build this future.

As the next trend comes, it will emit signals, telling us that we are in a transition phase. The rise of self-publishing is one of them. In the transition period, I'm expecting more and more authors will follow the *Harvard Business Review's* "preview approach" in which it provides multiple versions of its book, including what I call the "essentials" and the "complete" versions.

The "essentials" version is a short book, containing only one or two chapters delivering only the central message. Those chapters represent the best parts of the book—the golden nuggets. You should note that the deliberate reading approach complements, and perhaps even predicts, the "essentials" version of a book. The "complete" version provides much more information in case the reader wants to learn more, but the added information is optional.

This multi-version approach enables the machine learning system to start tagging chapters with extra data, such as topic, concept, and idea, and to index those chapters more efficiently. At the same time, readers get better use of their time as they can easily navigate, pick, and choose what's best for them.

IT'S YOUR TURN

The world knowledge is constantly accelerating, and you have learned the essential reading technique that could differentiate you from the crowd. You don't have to be a speed-reader or have to sacrifice your precious family-time to read. By following the simple steps and guidelines in this book, you can rest assured that you are set on the right course for big opportunities.

I revealed the three myths that can put an end to years of wasteful reading. We then went deep into the better approach—**deliberated reading**. By incorporating all four aspects—**selective focus, repetition, balance,** and **getting in the right gear**—you can turn reading into your secret recipe for reaching the top—and staying there.

You even learned the tricks to form reading habits and organize your reading into a bigger, personal life philosophy. In your next rereading of this book, be sure to refer back to the "Cheat Sheet" in chapter 2 for a reminder of the simple daily steps of deliberated reading.

With all the information in this book, I hope you will build your own home library and soon join the club of successful people. Whatever your goals are, you are now armed with the tools, systems, and strategies to get there.

So go forth, practice deliberated reading at every opportunity, and have fun doing so.

ACKNOWLEDGEMENTS

I began outlining this book in the summer of 2015 and submitted the first full draft to Kindle on Nov 1st, a five-month journey I certainly couldn't have navigated without help. Lots of it.

Family comes first. Without the love and support of my wife Kim, this book won't be what it is. I had a benefit of working with a great designer Haresh, who put together a stunning cover for my book. It is also my pleasure to have an irreplaceable editor - Nancy Pile, who did the hard work to turn a bunch of text into a "book".

Special thanks to my coach Sean Sumner and the SPS folks, who put together the great program to help me finish the book. I also want to show my gratitude to my accountability buddy Thuy Pham for checking in with me for many weeks.

Made in the USA
Lexington, KY
20 September 2016